I have known E
fact, Beth was and helped me write several of my own books, including *Fashioned to Reign*.

In her new book, *Dream Changer: Transform Your Nightmares into Victories, Find Help for Bad Dreams, and Win Spiritual Battles in Your Sleep*, Beth takes us on a powerful journey from victims of the night to victors in Christ. Through her own unique experiences, along with Biblical truths, Beth teaches us how to partner with God to defeat the fear and torment rooted in bad dreams. She equips us to defeat the enemy of our souls and empowers us to thrive in every epic season of life.

If you long to know how to win the battle against fear, anxiety, and confusion that nightmares can cause, this book is for you. I highly recommend it!

— KRIS VALLOTTON, SENIOR ASSOCIATE
LEADER, BETHEL CHURCH, REDDING, CA AND
CO-FOUNDER OF BETHEL SCHOOL OF
SUPERNATURAL MINISTRY; AUTHOR OF SEVERAL
BOOKS, INCLUDING *THE SUPERNATURAL WAYS OF
ROYALTY, SPIRIT WARS, AND POVERTY, RICHES
AND WEALTH*

"Beth Chiles's book, *Dream Changer*, is a must have in your spiritual arsenal. We've previously had the knowledge to cancel the effects of bad dreams but now God has given Beth missing keys to partner with Him to turn those dreams for our good. I, personally, have experienced life changing fruit and answers to prayer from implementing the revelation Beth shares practically in her book. I highly recommend this life changing book!"

— ANNIE BLOUIN, AUTHOR OF *EVERLASTING DOORS: WHEN THE SUPERNATURAL PENETRATES AMERICAN POLITICS; EVERLASTING PROPHETIC: BRIDGING HEAVEN TO EARTH; AND PROPHETIC REVELATION: KEYS TO SPIRITUAL MATURITY*

"In *Dream Changer,* Beth shares through her personal journey, practical and solid keys for dealing with torment and pain in your dream life. God is speaking all the time; his main language is not English. In this book, Beth will prepare you to transform your tormenting dream experience to one of increased blessings, peace, joy and strength in your life and your relationship with God."

— Kristi Graner, Founder and Director of Dare to Believe Ministries

dream
changer

BETH CHILES

dream
changer

Transform Your Nightmares into Victories,
Find Help for Bad Dreams, and
Win Spiritual Battles in Your Sleep

Dwell Book Press

Some names and details of stories included in this book have been changed in order to protect identities.

To everyone who has suffered from bad dreams and did not know what to do with them— may you find hope and courage in the pages of this book.

CONTENTS

ACKNOWLEDGMENTS

My husband Gary. There is no one I would rather be on this adventure of life with than you. You are my biggest cheerleader; without you I would not have finished this book. I love you so much!

My children Lily and Leland. You made all my dreams of having a family come true. I love you *and* I like you. I'm so grateful that I get to be your mom. And I can't forget our sweet dog Lizzie. Getting a dog was the best decision we've ever made.

My parents, Jack and Sharon Johnson. Thank you for giving me a rich and priceless heritage in the Lord. You have always gone above and beyond to be there for me and my family. I love you. And to my siblings, Susan and David, and Mark and Julie. You are the best!

My in-laws, Larry Chiles and Sharon Cunningham. You both would do anything to help someone in need.

I love you and am so fortunate to have you in my life. And to my brothers and sisters-in-law. Victoria, Deanna, Hollie, Brad and your families. So thankful for you!

My prayer team. Sharon, Annie, Anne, Caron, Donna, Fern, Leeann, Linda, Kay, Nancy, Pam, and Yina. Thank you for praying for me throughout the years, but especially for this book. It made all the difference in the world!

Kris and Kathy Vallotton. You prayed for me through life's ups and downs. You took a chance on me over ten years ago when you hired me. You were relentless in your belief in me, and I learned from you to never give up.

Team Chiles. You know who you are. The best team ever!

Cindy McGill. What you are doing with dreams to reach the lost is breathtaking. Your courage and strength in the face of adversity from every side is inspiring. Thank you for your friendship.

Kristi Graner. Your dream classes changed my life. Thank you for your friendship and wisdom.

INTRODUCTION

For most of my life, nightmares were a constant struggle, and I had no idea what to do about them. I felt
powerless, hopeless, and afraid. I struggled for years,
and there was little hope that things would ever
change. It felt as though this would be a normal part of
my life and dreaded every time I would wake up from
one. Was there any way to make them stop? Were there
any solutions to this fear?

Then one day, my dream life was turned upside
down. It felt as if blinders dropped from my eyes, and I
could see clearly. For the first time in my life, I realized
I didn't have to be a victim of my bad dreams. The
good news is neither do you.

Throughout the Bible, God uses dreams to speak to
His people—and He still does! But what happens
when you have a bad or confusing dream? Can God

still use it as well? The answer is yes! We don't have to be the target of the enemy's harassing dreams anymore. There is hope!

If you or someone you love suffers from bad dreams, there is an answer. You no longer have to live with fear, helplessness, or confusion. With God's help, you can transform your nightmares into victories, find help for bad dreams, and win spiritual battles in your sleep.

1

NIGHT TERROR

It was an average late-fall day. In Arizona, that means a welcome break from the sweltering summer heat. My husband, who was a property manager, and I, a legal assistant, went to work at our jobs early that morning as usual. At the end of the day, we fought the bumper-to-bumper Phoenix traffic on the way home, cooked dinner together, probably watched a little TV, and then went off to bed.

I fell into a deep sleep fairly quickly, only to stumble into a terrible dream shortly after. It was the kind of dream you remember forever. Even though I was asleep, it seemed like I was wide awake. Out of nowhere, I felt an evil presence envelop me like I had never sensed before. Its sulfur breath quietly exhaled next to my face, invisible and yet all-consuming. My skin prickled with fear, and a ball of terror formed in my stomach.

Time slowed to a crawl as my pulse pounded in my ears and became the only sound I could hear. I struggled to move but was paralyzed by fear. It was as if a ton of weight was lying on top of me, pressing me into the bed and crushing out my breath. I felt like I was drowning, which thwarted my feeble attempts to cry out. I fought desperately to wake up but felt trapped in a zone that I couldn't escape.

I fought desperately to wake up but felt trapped in a zone that I couldn't escape.

When I finally awoke, my eyes sprung open, but terror was thick in the room, and I still couldn't move. I was gasping for breath, my heart was racing uncontrollably, and I was trembling and sweating profusely. What in the world just happened? I opened my mouth in an attempt to call out to my husband for help, but I couldn't speak. When I could finally move again, I stumbled out of bed and into our tiny living room, fell on my knees, and cried out to God for help.

Eventually, the terror faded away that night, and I went back to sleep, and over the next few days, life seemingly went back to normal. Except that it didn't. About a week later, I started having terrible abdominal pains—the kind where I was doubled over, desperately clutching my side and gasping for breath, waiting for the agony to subside.

Over and over, the spasms would come in waves, relentlessly pounding day and night. The doctor thought it could be a kidney infection and put me on several rounds of antibiotics, but nothing changed. Weeks and months passed, but the pain only worsened.

Desperate to find an answer to my agony, I went to doctor after doctor. Finally, I was admitted to the hospital and had emergency surgery for a ruptured appendix, but an unusual kind. It was a slow leak, and poison had been seeping into my body for months. The surgeon was astounded that I was still alive. Over the next few months, I slowly recovered from the surgery. Except that I didn't.

Every time I ate, my stomach would cramp, leaving me in gut-wrenching pain. I continued to lose weight, eventually shrinking to eighty-five pounds. I was wasting away, and the doctors again couldn't find a cause. Eating and drinking anything, including water, left me in agony. Finally, after enduring months of medical tests I was diagnosed with Crohn's Disease, a debilitating disease with no known cure.

Is it possible that all of this pain and suffering stemmed from that dream I had almost a year before? I don't believe it was a coincidence.

Dreams can be a picture of what is happening in the spiritual dimension. God is giving us a glimpse into another realm, a realm that is more real than we know. There's a war going on between good and evil, death and life, terror and peace—and your dreams may be a part of it. I believe God is waking us up to the truth that we can fight spiritual battles in our dreams.

If you sense that your dreams are part of that war, or if you feel like you have been through a battle upon waking up, please know that you do not have to let the enemy win when you have a bad dream! Instead, you can be ready for any evil plans that come your way and win these battles.

But what can you do when you encounter these dreams? Is there any way to combat nightmares—such as being chased by a bear or an alligator, losing a purse, wallet, teeth, or hair, or fighting a losing battle against an unknown enemy? These are some of the most common bad dreams people struggle with, yet many people do not know what to do with them.

For most of my life, I was only aware of two options: to pray that the bad dreams would go away or to ignore them. That was it; there weren't any other alternatives. Practicing the "ignorance is bliss" motto, I would shake off these bad experiences, hoping they would go away—and they would for a while. Except that they didn't.

As early as I can remember, I've had bad dreams. From the time I was a little girl, I would often dream about tornadoes, storms, and fires. When I awoke, I would run to my mom who would hold me in her arms and comfort me, and we would pray together that the bad dream would go away. Of course, at age five, I had no idea what else to do, and neither did my mom.

Interestingly, I didn't realize at first that many of these dreams came true. For example, several times, I dreamed about tornadoes hitting a relative's home, and not long after, tragedy of one kind or another would strike their family. It would be anything from a severe illness to an extensive electrical fire to a serious car accident.

God is waking us up to the truth that we can fight spiritual battles in our dreams

When I was four or five years old, I dreamed that a house in my neighborhood caught fire. Later that day, fire trucks screamed by and stopped at that house to put out a fire. No one was hurt, fortunately, but the house did sustain significant damage.

Instead of being excited about these dreams coming true, it made me *more* afraid to dream. In my childlike understanding, I equated my bad dreams as the cause of these tragedies. This triggered an internal response that made me not want to dream at all! How terrifying for a child to see something bad come true after experiencing a dream.

Throughout my adult years, I still had nightmares —not on a daily occurrence, but often enough to be troublesome. For example, one disturbing dream I had repeatedly was that I was drowning, head underwater, unable to come up for air. My arms would flail as I struggled to escape, to no avail. I tried to speak and pray, but no words would come out. I would wake up in a panic, gasping for breath, trying to steady my racing heartbeat. Even though I would pray over and over for peace, read my Bible, and listen to worship songs on repeat, nothing stopped this dream from coming back time and time again.

Over time, I began to realize that a battle was raging inside, but I didn't know how to put words to it. A deep feeling of hopelessness and despair would come over me as I tried to escape these dreams. I longed to find answers but didn't know which way to turn.

Later, as I matured, I came to realize that my dreams were not the cause of these tragedies. God was warning me that something terrible might happen, and I needed to pray—and not just a generic prayer but one with a God-given strategy. Realizing this changed my life! Before this, I wanted to shut my dream life down. I was tired of struggling with the fear bad dreams would cause.

In talking with other people who dream, I was surprised to hear the same response—they struggled with bad dreams, especially the ones that came true. They were intimidated by bad dreams, not knowing what to do when they had them. They struggled with the same fear as I had. Was there any strategy or hope, or was this just the way it was going to be? It seemed easier not to dream at all than to have bad ones and feel helpless in the process. Yet, I also knew that dreams were important, so I didn't want to give up on them either.

One of the main reasons I'm writing this book is to give people hope that there is something you can do with your bad dreams. You and I are not helpless! There is a way to fight and bring about God's desire in our dreams.

2

LEARNING TO LISTEN

I'm not sure how this theory became a generally accepted belief in society, but everyone I knew assumed that suffering from bad dreams was merely a normal part of life. We didn't give any thought to other options. Sadly, we prayed that we would forget the dream and go on with life and hope we didn't have any more of them.

However, as I grew older and learned more about dreams, my reaction to them started to change. I heard other people's stories about how they prayed into their dreams, which encouraged me to start changing my perspective. Instead of hopelessness, I experienced a sense of working *with* God instead of being a victim or passive participant.

Encouraged, I began to pray through my dreams as if they were prayer requests. For instance, if I dreamed about a fire, I prayed for the situation and asked the Lord to be with the people whom the tragedy affected. Likewise, a dream about a storm over someone's home prompted prayers for minimal damage. That's about as far as my immature prayer life went, but it was a start in the right direction.

As time went on, there were seasons when I would dream regularly, but other times I would go months at a time without dreaming at all. There didn't seem to be any rhyme or reason to when I would dream a lot and when I wouldn't. But during one particular time in my life, I had several powerful dreams that came true almost immediately and made me want to learn even more.

Everyone I knew assumed that suffering from bad dreams was merely a normal part of life

One pivotal dream I had during this time involved people at my work. In my dream, we were having an afternoon picnic at a nearby park. We were all walking together on a path, but soon one of the key managers veered off and took a Y in the trail, separating from the rest of the group. Then I woke up.

That same day, this manager called me aside and told me she was giving her notice that day and was leaving the company in two weeks. I was shocked! Talk about instant results.

It was an exciting time, and while this dream didn't have anything specific to pray about, it got my attention that God was speaking to me through my dreams. My hunger for learning more about this field intensified.

In another dream, I was in a friend's garage playing games with their three children, but when I looked outside, flames had engulfed their house. The kids noticed the fire but reacted nonchalantly. They weren't panicked or worried about it at all; they barely looked up and continued playing their game. Then I woke up.

It was a troubling dream, so I prayed about it. But soon, it became a distant memory. A couple of weeks later, I heard that children's parents were having severe marriage problems. I was shocked when I heard the news because there was absolutely no indication of their struggles from the outside. I remember talking to the Lord, expressing my disappointment that He didn't warn me about the situation, especially since I was close with the family.

A few minutes later, it dawned on me. The Lord *did* tell me about it by giving me the dream that their house was on fire! I'm embarrassed to admit it now, but in my youth, I was more excited about the dream than I was heartbroken over their marriage struggles. I prayed for them, but I was immature and didn't have the level of compassion I should have had for this family that was struggling so deeply.

As time went on, I read many dream interpretation books, which were fascinating and crucial in knowing what various things in my dreams meant. I devoured dozens of books and learned the meaning of numbers, animals, vehicles, and more.

I discovered that God loves to use dreams to speak to people. For example, in the Bible, God used a dream to save Jesus' life when He told Joseph to flee King Herod, the Hitler of the day. Job also talks about dreams, saying, "In a dream, a vision of the night, when sound sleep falls on men, while they slumber in their beds, then He opens the ears of men, and seals their instruction" (Job 33:15–16 NASB).

My favorite dreamer in the Bible is Joseph in the Old Testament. He was a young man—only about seventeen years old—when he dreamed about the sheaths of grain and then the sun, moon, and stars bowing down to him. In his immaturity, he announced it to anyone who would listen, which lead to friction in his relationship with his brothers. They weren't quite ready to bow down to their spoiled younger brother, but yet, in the end, his dreams came true—despite the turmoil that ensued between the time of his dreams and their fulfillment.

These Biblical examples are only the tip of the iceberg of how God uses dreams to speak to people, and in studying them, I started to understand the basics of dream language. Instead of hoping for a bad dream to go away or offering a generalized prayer over the situation, my dreams became a source of directed intercession and targeted prayer. For instance, knowing that alligators in dreams refer to gossip allowed me to pray specifically for people or situations in my dreams that might be centered on or burdened by gossip.

My discovery of how God speaks through dreams was a huge step in the right direction, and I felt my heart connecting to Him in a new and exciting way. Dreams became a catalyst to a closer relationship with the Lord— a secret language between the two of us. He would speak to me in dreams, and I would search out the meaning and pray about them. It was an exciting time!

> *Dreams became a catalyst to a closer relationship with the Lord*

But I still had so much to learn.

Over the next twenty years or so, I had peaks and valleys in my dream life. There were seasons when I regularly had powerful dreams, and others when I went months and even years with only an occasional dream. I continued to read books on dream interpretation, but nothing significant changed in the way I handled them. I thought this was all there was to dreaming: you have a dream, and then you pray about it.

Little did I know that I was about to have an encounter that would change everything I thought I knew about dreams.

3

CHANGING DREAMS: WHAT IS THIS?

I t was a difficult time in my life. We had moved back to the Midwest and were living with my parents in their basement. We love my parents, but it's just not where we expected to be at that time in our lives. On top of that, my husband's new business didn't take off like we were hoping it would. I was working full time, and that was going well, but it wasn't enough to where we could afford to buy our own place. I felt trapped in our situation with no way out.

One day, my mom came home and told me that she had purchased tickets to a women's conference and asked if I wanted to go with her. I didn't want to go— going to a conference was the last thing I wanted to do. I had been to dozens of conferences and was too depressed to sit through another one. But since she already bought a ticket for me, I felt obligated to go.

Reluctantly, and with no expectation at all, I went to the event with my mom. That evening, Cindy McGill was the speaker. I had never heard of her before, but she had a ministry of bringing teams into dark places —like Burning Man and pornography conventions— to minister to broken people by interpreting their dreams.

"I will stay in this basement forever if I can have that kind of relationship with you."

As she told her story, I was undone by the profound effect she was having on the lost. People were being set free by her unconditional love, and she was connecting with them through dreams that they didn't understand. What stood out to me more was that she was having a blast doing it! My Christian life felt stagnant and boring, and Cindy was a breath of fresh air to my dry and parched soul.

That night after returning home from the conference, I knelt on the floor next to my bed and poured out my heart to the Lord: "I will stay in this basement forever if I can have that kind of relationship with you." It had been years since I had dreamed regularly, and I was ready for an adventure with God. The way Cindy was helping people was the most fun I had seen in a long time.

Surprisingly, two days later, I started dreaming again. After several years of hardly dreaming at all, the floodgates suddenly opened up. I had profound dreams almost every night, and sometimes several dreams a night—I was so excited! I had my special love language with God back again. My spirit felt like it was awakening after a long, dark sleep.

Because I had studied dreams for many years, I had a good foundation for understanding some of them. But because I was having so many dreams, a new kind of problem surfaced. With so much information coming at me through these dreams, I needed to advance to another level in my dream interpretation skills, and quickly! I had never experienced anything like this.

One of the main challenges I faced was discerning the source of my dreams: Which dreams were from the Lord versus the enemy? Which dreams were natural, caused by something I watched or read the night before? I had so many questions.

Likewise, some of my dreams were confusing, involving things of which I had never read. What did it mean if I dreamed about someone breaking into my house? What about a ship or a jumbo jet? What about being in a war or if a sniper was coming after me?

These questions put me on a treasure hunt to find answers. I was like a detective hot on a case. I dug all of my dream books out of storage and searched for clues.

I investigated many books on dream interpretation, including Cindy McGill's book *What Your Dreams are Telling You*[1] and *The Prophet's Dictionary* by Paula Price.[2] Many more that have helped me along the way —I have included them in the recommended resources at the end of this book.

After years of hardly dreaming at all, the floodgates suddenly opened up

I also combed the internet for information on classes I could take on dream interpretation. In this process, one of the most helpful tools I discovered was John Paul Jackson's course on dreams called Understanding Dreams and Visions.[3] John Paul Jackson, who passed away in 2015, was a forerunner in teaching dream interpretation and wrote many books on the subject. He had over thirty years of study and practical experience, impacting millions of people through his television appearances, books, courses, and speaking engagements. Check out his ministry Streams Ministries International[4] for more information.

Another resource I came across in my hunt for information was located in the city where I lived. Kristi Graner, whose ministry is called Dare to Believe,[5] was a huge blessing—and she lived right in my neighborhood. Kristi has extensive ministry experience and training on dream interpretation and had even traveled around the world with John Paul Jackson's ministry.

As it so happened, when I came across her website, she was advertising a dream interpretation class that was only a couple of weeks away, so I signed up immediately. Her class covered several topics, such as developing the ability to hear God through dreams, how to recognize which dreams are important and which are not, and methods of organizing and tracking dreams.

Her class was fantastic, and I learned so much from her. She also has several great resources available on her website, and I encourage anyone interested in learning more about interpreting dreams to check them out.

Here's where things became interesting and changed the course of my dream life. A few weeks after I attended Kristi Graner's class, she hosted a special event with a speaker named Recie Saunders. Recie teaches dream interpretation and had been on staff with John Paul Jackson's ministry for many years. He travels and speaks around the world to this day.

At his seminar, Recie taught a class geared toward children, and I attended it with my two kids. His teaching on children's dreams and their nightmares was fascinating! During this seminar, he mentioned something that piqued my curiosity. It was nothing I had heard of before, and yet his testimonies about it were amazing.

A few weeks later, as I was battling to interpret some of my tough dreams, the Lord reminded me of Recie's stories of how he helped children with their nightmares (which I will share in a moment). Instantly, I realized that there was something there for me! As the Holy Spirit helped me to process and adapt these principles into my dream life, I started to call this "re-dreaming."

Recie taught that when a child has a nightmare, instead of trying to make the bad dream go away by running to mom and dad in fear, there is a better option. Parents need to teach the child that they have the power to do something about it instead of being afraid. The goal is for children to learn how to fight the enemy instead of being a victim.

Recie encourages the child to choose a superhero that he loves, someone like Spiderman, Wonder Woman, Captain Marvel, or Captain America. What child doesn't love to pretend to be a hero? I remember racing down the hallway in my childhood home, trying to make my cape float behind me, and jumping off the sofa pretending to fly. A superhero is easy for a child to imagine.

Next, he instructs the child to pray and then use those superhero strengths in their imagination to defeat the enemy, which empowers them to overcome the villain in their dream.

If a child has a nightmare about someone chasing him, the parent should start by encouraging them to use their imagination to remember the dream. Then they use these superpower strengths to overcome the

Children become empowered to defeat the enemy

bad guys. In other words, as they see the bad guy coming in their dream, they can use Spiderman's web shooter or Wonder Woman's lasso to neutralize the adversary.

This solution may seem simple, but it's very effective and will help the child realize that they are partnering with the Lord to overcome whatever is bothering them in their sleep. They no longer have to run away in fear. Instead, they can learn the truth that Paul declares in Romans that "in all these things we are more than conquerors through him who loved us" (Romans 8:37 NIV).

In testimony after testimony, when parents have done this with their kids, they have seen amazing things happen. Bad dreams no longer plague many kids who had been tormented with nightmares. What is exciting to see is that their children become empowered to defeat the enemy by themselves without the help of mom or dad. Recie explains this in more detail in his book, *A Parent's Guide to Understanding Children's Dreams and Nightmares.*[6] He tells several stories of children who were no longer afraid of the dark or fearful of dreaming because they had taken control and learned to fight for themselves.

When I heard this teaching, I thought it was a powerful way for kids to overcome their nightmares and show them their spiritual authority. However, I wasn't quite sure how it applied to me and didn't give it much thought after that. That's where I left it until a couple of weeks later when the Lord opened my eyes to something more.

4

PIONEER SETTLEMENT DREAM

A couple of weeks after the dream seminar on children's nightmares, I was reviewing some of my dreams and came across one that I had a few weeks earlier, which I called the "Pioneer Settlement" dream. When I had the dream, I felt like it was significant, but didn't know what it meant. But on this particular morning, it caught my eye. It was as if the Lord pointed it out to me in a unique way, and it ended up dramatically changing the way I look at dreams forever.

I dreamed I was living in a pioneer settlement in the Old West. It was a small, primitive group of homes and businesses with about 75–100 people living there. What stood out was a large two-story house in the center of the settlement.

Somehow, we found out that a gang of bandits was coming to kill us and steal everything we owned, so we constantly watched for the enemy, looking for signs of movement on the horizon. Far off in the distance, we saw a stranger riding a horse toward us, so a few men from the settlement rode out to meet him. It turned out to be a lookout from the enemy, and we knew the gang was close.

In a panic, we scurried around, gathering everyone together in the large house. I was inside comforting the women and children, explaining what heaven was like. I talked about the streets of gold, the beautiful mansions, and seeing Jesus. As the bandits were closing in, I ushered everyone to the basement of the house. I told them that death was just like stepping into a new dimension, and there was nothing to be afraid of. Then I woke up.

My heart was pounding as I wrote down the dream with as many details as I could remember. Immediately, I pondered all the different parts of the story. Questions flooded my mind: What did this dream mean? Was my family in danger? How do I pray about this one?

Soon I fell back to sleep, but the dream stayed with me for a day or so. Once the initial emotion of the dream wore off, I concluded that I was satisfied with the way I handled myself in the dream. After all, didn't I comfort the women and children as death loomed near? Wasn't I leading them to the safest place in the house? Didn't I point them toward Jesus and heaven as the end drew near? I was a bit proud of the pastoral and comforting way I acted in my dream.

I didn't pursue the dream any further, and pretty much forgot about it until this particular morning. Out of nowhere, I felt the Holy Spirit highlight this dream. As I was reading through it in my journal, it was like a lightbulb went off inside of me and I saw what was wrong with the way I was looking at it.

In my dream, I was going to let the enemy plunder and kill us without a fight! What was I thinking? Not once did it occur to me to fight the bandits and rescue the people with me. Instead, I was passive, thinking that comfort alone was a great spiritual response. Instead, *When this revelation hit me, it was as if the blinders were taken off and I could see clearly* the enemy loved the fact that he could ride in without any resistance and have his way, destroying my life and the entire village with me.

When this revelation hit me, it was as if the blinders were taken off, and I could see clearly. My prideful, yet passive reaction to this dream was not how God wanted me to handle it. Something stirred inside of me! I realized that it wasn't too late to change.

Suddenly, the Holy Spirit connected the dots between Recie's teaching about children's nightmares and how I could use some of the same principles for my dreams. Recie taught that children could go back into their dreams and change them immediately when they had a nightmare. I began to use this concept in a little different way.

The Lord showed me that I could partner with Him in prayer for insight into my dreams. Then I could go back days, weeks, and even months later to change them into what God showed me. (I will explain this process in greater detail in the next chapter.)

I was shocked, excited, and scared at this revelation. Questions flooded my mind: Would it work? Was it possible to re-dream a dream and fight spiritual battles through them? Could dreams really be changed?

I was tired of being trapped as a helpless victim to bad dreams, with no real strategy to conquer the enemy. Encouraged by the Lord, but with these questions at the back of my mind, I decided to start on this new journey with Him to see what exciting things He would do.

With this in mind, I knew I had to change my Pioneer Settlement dream. I asked the Holy Spirit how to handle this attack from the enemy and how to fight back. Once I felt like the Lord told me what I should do, I closed my eyes and remembered the dream. Only this time, instead of heading to the basement to die, I imagined that I gathered the people around me and told them we were going to fight the enemy as I handed out weapons to each person. When we saw the bandits coming into view, we hit them with everything we had, and the enemy turned and ran away in defeat.

After I changed this dream, something inside of me was transformed. It was a life-changing moment! The authority of the Lord rose in me in a new way, and I discovered that I did not have to be a victim of bad dreams anymore. I don't have to let evil win! I began to walk in the knowledge that I could use my spiritual authority to fight the enemy, even in my dreams.

It was exciting to partner with the Lord to see what He wanted to do in my dreams. As I started doing this, I was amazed at the changes that started to happen in my life. I even changed a dream that altered the course of my family's life that I will share in Chapter 7.

In the next chapter, I will share what I have learned about how to re-dream dreams, and how you can do it too.

5

HOW TO CHANGE A DREAM

Changing a dream with the Holy Spirit opened up the door to a whole new way of looking at dreams! It taught me to look at spiritual warfare through a different lens. It's possible to be an active participant in dreams instead of a passive bystander. Although I don't believe every dream is spiritual warfare, I do think there is a lot more to dreams than most people realize.

Fighting battles in the Spirit is a normal part of the Christian life. Paul states clearly in Ephesians that "we are not struggling against human beings, but against the rulers, authorities and cosmic powers governing this darkness, against the spiritual forces of evil in the heavenly realm" (Ephesians 6:12 CJB). Spiritual forces affect believers whether they know it or not, and simply being aware of this fact helps define what the struggle is really about.

So how exactly do you change a dream? Over the past few years of prayer and study, I've narrowed the process down into three simple steps that work for me: write, pray, and re-dream.

Write

The first thing I do with all the dreams I have is write them down immediately before I forget them, either in the Notes app on my phone or in my dream journal. This might seem simple, yet it's vital. I give each one a title, which makes it easier to keep them organized and find them later.

Changing a dream with the Holy Spirit opened up the door to a whole new way of looking at dreams

I've learned the hard way that it's not a good idea to wait until morning to write them down. More times than I can count, I have forgotten dreams shortly after having them. There have been times when I woke up in the middle of the night from a dream and decided to wait until morning to record it. The dream was so clear and profound I was sure I wouldn't forget it, but when morning came, it was a foggy, distant memory. No matter how hard I searched my brain, I couldn't remember any of the details, and all was lost. It's worth it to take a few minutes and record them immediately!

One benefit of keeping a dream journal is that your dream history grows in depth over time as you record them. It is a great way to explore the seasons of life and gain insight into your destiny or make corrections in areas you may be struggling in.

To dig a little deeper into a dream's meaning, I use a journal format, which helps me break down the parts of a dream in an organized way. This layout helps me remember the dream and the key points, discern the meaning, connection to other dreams, and whether or not it needs changing. It is also important to have a space to sketch if something is difficult to describe.

To help facilitate this process, I created a dream journal, *The Dream Changer Journal*, which is available at www.bethchiles.net if you are interested in learning more. In it, I go into further detail with examples of each of these categories.

Pray

I want everything I do to be done in relationship with the Lord, and working through a dream is no different. So, when I sit down to process what I dreamed the night before, I first start by thanking Him for the dream, whether it is good or bad. We obviously like the good dreams, but the bad dreams are just as important —they both can reveal what is happening in the spiritual realm.

After thanking the Lord for the dream, I ask Him for the meaning. Even if I think I know the interpretation, I still talk to the Lord about it. Taking time to listen to the Holy Spirit can give meaning and direction that I wouldn't have had if I just plowed ahead with my own view.

My Pioneer Settlement dream (see Chapter 4) is a great example of how I was wrong with my initial interpretation. At first, I was satisfied with how I responded to the attack, which would have ended up with all of us dying. But later, in a lightbulb moment, I realized how apathetic I was to the oncoming invasion. Instead, if I had asked the Lord right away, I would have seen His perspective, which was to stand and fight. Once that realization struck me, I knew I could change this dream and destroy the plans of the enemy instead of being destroyed.

When you pray, you might be surprised that sometimes God will tell you not to change anything at all. Why would He do such a thing when the dream seems bad? It might be hard to understand, but God's ways are above man's (Isaiah 55:8–9), and you can trust Him to know what is best. It is far better to learn to listen to what the Holy Spirit is saying about your dreams than to do your own thing. This takes patience and practice.

Here is an interesting example that emphasizes the importance of this principle. Friends of ours were expecting a baby, and the father had a dream that a doctor was holding up their newborn baby boy in a hospital. In real life, they had planned a home birth, so this didn't make sense to him. He immediately wanted to change the dream to have a home birth, but when he prayed about it, the Holy Spirit told him *not* to change it. He didn't understand at all, but he trusted the Lord and left it alone.

Before the due date, some medical concerns forced them to go to the hospital to have the mother and baby checked out. The doctor diagnosed the mother with an abruptio placenta, which can be fatal to both mom and

Your dream history grows in depth over time as you record them

baby. But because they were already in the hospital, the doctor was able to save them both. The doctor told them that if they hadn't been in the hospital, they would have lost both the mother and the baby. This miracle solidified my friend's perspective about listening to the Lord when He says not to change a dream.

The funny thing is when the doctor came out to

talk to the father, he told him they had a baby girl. Because our friend had seen a baby boy in his dream, he questioned the doctor, "Are you sure it's not a boy?" (They did not find out beforehand whether it was a girl or a boy). The doctor replied, "Yes, I'm sure it's a girl." But as the doctor was speaking, the nurse interrupted him and exclaimed, "It's not a girl, it's a boy!"

It's not always God's desire for you to change your dream. This requires trust and patience when you know you can change it, but He says to wait. Because God is good, you can be confident in the fact that He knows what's best.

Change

Finally, after writing down the dream and praying about it to hear from the Lord on the best direction to take, it is time to change or re-dream the dream. It's simple, but it will take practice to gain confidence.

All I do is close my eyes and picture myself back in the dream. But instead of replaying the original dream in my mind, I change it to what I sense the Lord wants to do. By doing this, I am partnering with Him in this process of changing the dream.

That's it! It may only take a minute or two; it's not a long, drawn-out process. You don't have to go to sleep, and you might not feel anything. This isn't an emotional experience, and it is easy to think nothing has happened.

Most importantly, changing dreams is done by faith! God loves it when we walk by faith (Hebrews 11:6). When we pray, whether we are talking to Him about our finances, our health, or even our dreams, we believe that God hears us and will move on our behalf. This is the essence of faith.

Jesus declares that "if you have faith and do not doubt . . . you can say to this mountain, 'Go, throw yourself into the sea,' and it will be done" (Matthew 21:21 NIV). In other words, when we partner with Him in faith, we can see things change. If Jesus permits us to use our faith to move mountains, we can certainly use our faith and partner with Him to see our dreams changed!

Jesus goes on to state in the next verse, "And whatever you ask for in prayer, having faith and [really] believing, you will receive" (Matthew 21:22 AMPC). When we bring our dreams to the Lord in prayer, we are believing that He will accomplish the things that He inspires us to change in our dream. Through faith, Jesus gives us hope for something more than being a victim to our circumstances—whether it be in our life situations or the bad dreams we encounter.

It's important to remember that since our battle "is not against flesh and blood" (Ephesians 6:12 NIV) and "we live by faith, not by sight" (2 Corinthians 5:7 NIV), we won't always see results in the natural, even though we believe that something has shifted in the spiritual realm. Many times, prayer is to prevent things from happening, stopping the plans of the enemy. So, if prayer halts those plans, we won't necessarily see anything happen, because the plans are stopped. Changing dreams operates in the same way. Sometimes we don't see anything changed, but we sense a shift in our hearts and know something happened. Other times, we will see dramatic changes from changing dreams. (See Chapters 7 and 8 for several examples.)

If we can stop satan's schemes before they take place, we can prevent a lot of pain and suffering

Changing bad dreams to prevent attacks from the enemy reminds me of the movie *Minority Report* starring Tom Cruise. In this futuristic movie, gifted humans were part of an elite law enforcement squad called "Precrime." These agents would dream about crimes that were going to happen in the future so that they could be prevented. By using their dreams, this team virtually eliminated crime in their city. Even though this is science fiction, this concept is still intriguing to me.

What if we could do this with the Holy Spirit?

What if one of the reasons God gives us dreams is to warn us of upcoming attacks of the enemy so that we can pray to prevent it? If we can stop satan's schemes before they take place, we can prevent a lot of pain and suffering. This is the goal of re-dreaming: to stop the plans of the enemy so we can fulfill our destiny in God.

In the past, some of my dreams were scary, depressing, and discouraging because I didn't know what to do with them. I was at the mercy of my bad dreams, but now I realize that they have a purpose. These dreams give us clues as to what is happening in the spirit realm.

Now that I have a strategy in place to pray through and change these kinds of dreams, I actually welcome them because when the plans of the enemy are revealed, I can do something about them. I am no longer helpless, but a powerful warrior with the power to change them!

You will be too.

6

TIMING IS EVERYTHING

When I first started to change dreams, I would worry if I didn't know how to change the dream right away. I thought the sooner, the better— and the longer I waited, the less effective the change would be. But I soon found that this simply isn't true.

The timing of changing a dream can be immediate or after several weeks, months, or even longer. It all depends on when the Lord makes it clear on what direction to take. I've had occasions where I pondered a dream for several weeks (even months) before I knew what to do. There is no rush; it's not more effective to change it immediately. It is more important to change it how the Lord directs. The synergy between seeking the Lord, hearing what he says, and changing the dream accordingly can be life-changing.

Sniper Dream

The type of dreams that I tend to change immediately are the ones where a demonic force is attacking me. For instance, once I had a dream that I call the Sniper dream. I was on a bus in a huge parking garage with my husband. The driver was driving us down the ramp to leave and made a quick turn to take a shortcut to move us out of the ramp quicker. Out of nowhere, a demonic sniper started shooting at us from behind a cement barrier in the garage, but we escaped. Later we were driving our car, and the bus driver called to warn us that the same sniper was waiting for us up ahead on a bridge. Then I woke up.

I remember feeling urgency from the Lord as soon as I woke up, so I immediately prayed while typing it into my Notes app with as many details as I could remember. This was clearly an attack, but I wanted to see if the Holy Spirit would give any more information on how I should re-dream it.

After praying, I closed my eyes and remembered the dream. When the sniper came into view in the parking ramp, instead of shooting at us, his rifle jammed and exploded in his hands, thwarting the plans of the enemy. I felt it necessary to take immediate action because he came after us twice in my dream. Pay attention to multiples in dreams—like words spoken, images, or actions. Anything that happens more than once in a dream is a signal to be alert.

When it comes to changing dreams, it's essential to know that this is a journey of faith. Sometimes the results of re-dreaming a dream are evident, and sometimes they aren't. This is true with a lot of my dreams, including this Sniper dream. Even though I didn't see results in the natural, I believe that there were results in the supernatural, and the plans of the enemy were defeated before they could take place.

> *If we do not learn how to fight back, we will be powerless to overcome the enemy*

Violence

Some of these actions might seem violent, but this is a part of spiritual warfare. Please understand, I am not talking about fighting people but "spiritual forces of evil" (Ephesians 6:12). God calls believers to love people —even those who don't love them. Spiritual warfare is about destroying the plans of the enemy directed toward people.

Pretty much everyone has experienced the destructive attacks of the enemy, and are aware that he does not play nice. We need to pay attention to Peter's warning: "Be on your guard and stay awake. Your enemy, the devil, is like a roaring lion, sneaking around to find someone to attack" (1 Peter 5:8 CEV).

If we do not learn how to fight back, we will be powerless to overcome the enemy. He is after every area of our lives: health, emotions, family, finances—the list goes on. There is nothing off-limits to his realm of destruction.

The enemy does not ask if he's gone too far or wonder if he's done the wrong thing. He only has one thing on his mind: to ravage our lives with his evil plans. In describing the work of satan, Jesus declared that "The thief comes only to steal and kill and destroy" (John 10:10 NIV). This is his only objective—to ruin our lives. Thankfully, God's plan is different! Jesus continues this verse, stating: "I have come that they may have life, and have it to the full."

This is great news! We do not have to live in fear because Jesus has given us the authority and power to stand up and fight. Jesus loves to see the works of the enemy destroyed. John states that "The reason the Son of God appeared was to destroy the devil's work" (1 John 3:8).

And the news keeps getting better: He has even equipped us to join Him in overcoming the enemy! Why would we need to put on the armor of God described in Ephesians 6 if it's not to fight a battle? The enemy will try to destroy us if we do not overcome his schemes. We must rise and fight: we are warriors! We cannot be passive and let the enemy have his way with us. We can win this battle!

∼

Vulture Dream

A couple of years ago, I dreamed that my husband and I were having a cookout for a group of friends. In my dream, we were in our backyard, which was covered with lush green grass, pretty white lights crisscrossing the patio, and a rustic wood pergola for shade. In anticipation of our guests arriving soon, our grill was filled with chicken and burgers.

While the food was cooking, I turned away from the grill and walked inside the house to grab some tongs to turn the meat. When I came back outside, to my shock, there were dozens of black, hulking vultures on the grill violently ripping into the meat. I tried to shoo them away, waving my arms and yelling, but they didn't budge. Instead, they looked at me unblinkingly with a deathly stare and kept on eating. If I moved too close, they would lash out at me with their sharp beaks, flapping their wings and hissing threateningly. Then I woke up.

Instantly I knew this was a warning dream. I quickly grabbed my phone and wrote down the dream in my notes. I felt like God was giving me a glimpse of what was happening in the spiritual realm. Then I thanked the Lord for this dream. I have learned to be thankful even when it appears that a dream is negative because God is revealing the plans of the enemy. When I know what the enemy is up to, I can fight effectively.

I knew this dream needed to be changed, so I asked the Lord what He wanted me to do with it. I didn't hear anything right away, but after a day or so of pondering the dream, I felt like the Lord said that the enemy wanted to devour our provision. Stealing finances, destroying relationships, and causing sickness are just a few of satan's favorite methods of inflicting harm. It was evident we needed to thwart the enemy's plan before he destroyed us.

I felt like God was giving me a glimpse of what was happening in the spiritual realm

To change this dream, I felt like the Lord wanted to accompany me to confront the vultures. I closed my eyes and remembered the dream. I imagined myself coming out of the house, but this time, with the Lord by my side. He raised his hands toward the birds and said, "Be gone!" Instantly, every vulture vanished into thin air.

I immediately felt a sense of peace; the burden

from this dream had been lifted. Even though I waited a couple of days to change this dream, I knew that the Lord had overcome the plans of the enemy.

It is more important to hear what the Lord says than to jump in and change a dream based on feelings and desires. No matter how long it takes, it's always worth taking time to find out what the Lord is telling you.

Dreams from the Past

I have also seen powerful things happen in the area of childhood dreams. No dream is too old to change. Even if it's decades old, it's never too late to pray over them. Dreams from the past can be changed as easily as dreams in the present.

I've talked to several people who were tormented by dreams when they were young. The memories are so fresh it's like they dreamed it that day. One man I'll call Tony told of a recurring nightmare when he was a child.

In this dream, Tony was walking toward home on a neighborhood street. He would turn a corner, and suddenly, an evil man with a knife would jump out from behind a tree and chase him down the road. Tony would wake up in a cold sweat with his heart pounding. More than forty years later, he could still remember the fear he experienced from those dreams.

To cope with the fear, he had to shut down his dream life, which is not uncommon for kids who have bad dreams. The enemy loves it when this happens because he can cut off an avenue that God uses to speak to us. When we realize our authority in Christ, we can open up that path and allow God to communicate to us in our dreams once again.

I encouraged Tony to ask the Lord how he could re-dream that dream. God impressed him to imagine himself in the dream on his way home from school, except this time, he was prepared with a weapon. As he rounded the corner, he saw the evil man and chased him off before the man could come after him. Even after changing a dream decades later, Tony felt a sense of peace that he didn't realize was missing in his life.

If you have experienced nightmares as a child, ask the Holy Spirit how you can change those dreams to find victory over the enemy. Since there is no time-frame on changing dreams, try to remember nightmares from when you were young and take some time to talk to the Lord about them.

Dreams can be changed at any time. There is no time limit on what God can do when we invite Him into our dreams. Learning to hear His voice is the most critical aspect of re-dreaming. When we listen to what the Lord wants to do, we can turn our nightmares into victories!

7

THE DREAM THAT CHANGED MY LIFE

After re-dreaming the Pioneer Settlement dream, I was convinced that changing dreams worked. I knew I was on to something big, and my dream life would never be the same. Something changed in my spirit, and I knew I wasn't going to be a victim of bad dreams anymore.

Up until this point, I had changed a few dreams and could tell something shifted in the spirit, even though I hadn't seen "results" with my natural eyes. I wasn't discouraged by this because I have learned that prayer changes things in the spirit even if I don't always see things change immediately.

But all of this was about to change.

One day I was reviewing my dreams and came across one that caught my eye. It bothered me because I knew something needed changing, but I didn't know how or what needed to be done. I titled it the Invitation Dream. Little did I know that changing this dream would change my and my family's life.

One night I dreamed that I was in the basement of an office building looking for a box of invitations for a coworker. I found them in a banker's box on the floor and lugged them upstairs to give to him. As I approached his office door, he saw me coming and slammed the door in my face.

While precariously balancing the box in one hand, I struggled to open the door with the other. My coworker sneered, "Go put the invitations in the envelopes." Because of his arrogance, I was not happy about it, and we had a stare-down for about a minute. His look was one of contempt, and it felt like he was saying, "You better do what I say or else." I finally backed down, looked away, and began to work on the invitations. Then I woke up.

I was bothered by this dream for several weeks. For one thing, in real life, this guy would not behave that way, so this attitude in my dream did not make sense. It was totally out of character for him. I also wasn't sure what to do with this dream. Do I blow up the guy as if he were a demonic force like I was taught to do in spiritual warfare? Of course not. Do I continue the stare-down, and for how long? That would be ridiculous. How do I re-dream this one? I was stuck.

I spent a lot of time praying about this dream,

trying to hear the Holy Spirit. A few weeks later, it finally came to me! I felt like the Lord gave me a specific way to change this dream. Instead of rebuking or blowing him up, the Lord gave me clear direction on what to do.

Before I went to bed that night, I closed my eyes and remembered the dream. I imagined myself bringing the box of invitations to this guy, but instead of slamming the door, he took the box from me and said, "These invitations are for you; let me help you with them." Then I went to sleep. It only took about thirty seconds to change it.

Not only can changing dreams change things in the spiritual realm but also the natural world.

The next morning, in real life, I received a phone call from the same person in my dream. I hadn't talked to this person in quite a while, so his call took me by surprise. After a few minutes of small talk, he told me about a job opening that I instantly knew was the invitation in the dream. My mouth dropped open—I realized this had come about because I had changed the dream the night before.

I was stunned about the amazing opportunity he shared with me. But truthfully, I was even more excited that I had changed this dream less than twelve hours before he presented the position!

This job was a life-changing opportunity that altered the course of my and my family's life. Within thirty days of that phone call, we moved across the country with a new dream job that blessed our family immeasurably.

This experience cemented within me the reality of changing dreams. Not only can it change things in the spiritual realm but also the natural world. In the following chapter, I will share other examples from people I know who have changed dreams and seen incredible results.

8

DREAM CHANGING EXAMPLES

L et me share a few experiences from others of how they changed their bad dreams with guidance from the Lord, and saw amazing things happen.

A friend had a vivid dream that a devastating tornado was headed directly toward his brother's house, and he knew it was going to be destroyed. He asked the Lord how to re-dream this dream, believing that something was supposed to change. After hearing from God, he closed his eyes and remembered the dream. In his imagination, he threw off darkness and put on the armor of light. He then took a sword, ran straight toward the tornado, and thrust it directly into the center of the funnel, chopping at it to make sure it didn't harm the house.

Just one week later, out of nowhere, a huge tornado formed a block from where his brother lived and took a strange route. It was heading directly toward his brother's home, destroying all of the houses in its path. At a specific point, the tornado lifted, went over his brother's house, and disappeared. When our friend went to see the destruction, he noticed the tornado had lifted at the exact spot where he attacked the tornado in his dream. In fact, he had even drawn a picture in his journal of the specific location he saw the tornado lift!

The tornado lifted at the exact spot where he attacked the tornado in his dream

What are the chances of that? This was a great encouragement to our friend's faith that changing dreams works.

Another friend was expecting a baby, and the husband had a dream that something terrible happened to the baby during childbirth. When the husband awoke, he sought the Lord and asked for wisdom on what to do with this dream. The Lord impressed upon him to change the dream so the birth would be problem-free, and the baby would be born full of life. He wisely did not share this dream with his wife ahead of time because he did not want her to be afraid or experience negative emotions during the birth.

Weeks later, when they were delivering the baby,

they learned the cord was wrapped around his neck and he was not breathing. The midwife started to panic, but our friend reassured her that everything would be okay. Soon the baby took a breath. He lived and is strong and healthy to this day.

Because he had changed his dream according to what the Lord told him, he knew he had won the battle in the spirit. He had faith during the crisis that God was in control, and he had peace about the outcome.

Another friend dreamed that her husband was in the Army serving overseas in the desert, many years before they married. He was missing most of both feet due to an explosion. Because of his handicap, he could only work at a fast-food restaurant for minimum wage.

When she woke up, she was convinced she needed to change this dream. In real life, her husband had always struggled to find a job that was a good fit, and he frequently switched jobs trying to find something he liked. She talked to God about what He wanted to do in this situation, and here is how she changed her dream.

She closed her eyes and remembered the dream, but when she saw her husband's feet, she invited Jesus into the dream and asked Him to heal them. Jesus stretched out His hands and made them completely whole.

Within two months of that dream, he was offered his dream job and has been working at that place for many years now. She believes this was a direct result of changing her dream and believing by faith that God had healed her husband.

God loves to change dreams—and our lives

Another man I know dreamed he was being harassed by the Joker from the Batman movies. In the dream, the Joker was circling him menacingly, sneering and jabbing at him while laughing maniacally. Although my friend tried to get away, he couldn't escape.

When he awoke, he prayed about it and knew that this dream needed to be changed immediately. There was nothing going on in his life that he knew of that might have caused this dream—he wasn't involved in any visible conflict. He closed his eyes and remembered the dream. Instead of the Joker tormenting him, he lassoed him with a rope and asked the Lord to come and take care of the situation.

That same day, he was offered a promotion at his job that was perfect for him. Later he learned there was a huge debate about who would be offered this position. He believes the Lord gave him that dream so he could fight the enemy and fulfill his destiny.

A woman on my prayer team dreamed she was in a house with a white door at the end of a hallway. She felt that she was supposed to open the door and go through it. Stepping through the doorway, she walked into a huge, pitch-black cave with a dark and fearful presence. Instantly frightened, she turned and fled, quickly closing the door behind her.

When she woke up, she asked the Lord for protection and the meaning of the dream. She felt He was telling her to go back and change the dream, but she didn't understand right away what he wanted her to do. Trusting God to lead her, she closed her eyes and went back into the dream. When she opened the door, she realized she had a stick of dynamite in her hands with the fuse lit. She let it go, and it exploded bright light everywhere!

Immediately, she realized the dark cave represented a place in her soul that was filled with fear, the result of an issue in her past. As the light was permeating the entire cave from the explosion, she knew she was immediately healed from a past trauma. She thanks the Lord for the power of God to change dreams!

God loves to change dreams—and our lives. In the next chapter, I'll point out some principles I have learned not to do in this process. Just as it is important to learn what to do, it is just as important to learn what *not* to do when changing dreams.

9

WHAT NOT TO DO

I love the show, *What Not to Wear*. The show revolves around changing people's wardrobes from frumpy to fabulous. The hosts, Stacy and Clinton, ambush some poor soul who has been secretly nominated by friends or family members. These targets are in desperate need of a fashion makeover, and Stacy and Clinton came to the rescue. In the show, they point out what not to wear, offering basic principles to avoid when choosing a wardrobe. The transformations are nothing short of miraculous, and the clients are sent home with a list of dos and don'ts so they can continue to make good fashion decisions.

In the same way that Stacy and Clinton had fashion principles for what not to wear, here is my list of guidelines for "What Not to Do" when changing dreams.

Don't Manipulate God

An essential guideline for changing dreams is not to manipulate God. God is so good, and He loves you so much that you do not have to try to manipulate Him to get what you need. Let that truth sink into the core of your being, and it will guide every decision you make. The purpose of re-dreaming is not to fulfill selfish ambitions but to help fulfill your destiny in the Lord.

God is so good that you do not have to manipulate Him to get what you need

If you are facing a difficult situation, you may be tempted to re-dream dreams in a way to get what you want or to ensure your needs are met. But the Lord's ways and purposes are infinitely better than anything imaginable. The goal is to find out what His will and direction is in every situation and trust Him for the results.

The Bible encourages you to "Trust in the Lord with all your heart and lean not on your own understanding; in all your ways submit to him, and he will make your paths straight" (Proverbs 3:5–6). Likewise, you are fighting a battle against evil, so stay focused on the goodness of God, and trust Him to meet all of your needs (Philippians 4:19).

Don't randomly pray about what you want, but

instead, ask the Lord what *He* wants, and wait until you hear. For example, if you dream that you lost your purse or wallet, don't change it to where you win the lottery. If changing dreams worked like that, everyone would have won the jackpot by now.

Changing dreams isn't a method to fulfill greedy aspirations; the purpose is to fight the enemy who wants to keep you from fulfilling God's purposes in life by wreaking havoc in your world. If the Lord prompts you to pray for a million dollars, by all means, go for it! There is nothing wrong with being blessed financially. But don't be greedy. This is a walk of faith, and the Lord will take care of you in every area of your life.

Changing dreams is not a way to control God. God gives clues into the supernatural through dreams, and it is our responsibility—and even joy—to discern what he is trying to tell us. When we stay away from manipulation, we can win the war in our dreams and fulfill the purposes of God for our lives.

Don't Change the Dream When God Says "No"

When we ask the Lord what He wants to do with a dream, He will sometimes tell us to leave it alone, which might not make sense. But His ways are higher than our ways (Isaiah 55:9). We might see a situation negatively, but God has a different point of view. The key is to listen to what the Lord is saying and trust him because he knows what is best for us.

When my friend in Chapter 5 dreamed his baby was born in a hospital, even though he and his wife had planned to have a home birth, his initial response was to change the dream. But when he listened to the Lord, he knew he wasn't supposed to change it. Thankfully, the baby was born in the hospital just like he dreamed—if he hadn't been, the baby and mom could have died because of a serious medical issue they were facing.

Listen to and obey God when he says not to change a dream. He wants us to fulfill our destiny more than we do! Because we know how good God is, we can confidently hope in Him and trust Him when it might not make sense.

Don't Fight Against People

Don't be mad at the people in your dreams. I've mentioned this before, but it is worth repeating. Our struggles are not against people but spiritual forces of evil (Ephesians 6:12). If you have a bad dream about someone, it doesn't necessarily mean that person is evil. He or she could represent something else in your life.

Have you ever had a nightmare about your husband or wife—the kind where you wake up mad at them? Don't attack them in your re-dream, even if you want to. Pray about it and ask the Lord what to do.

Many years ago, I dreamed I was talking to my husband, but he wasn't listening to me. In fact, he outright ignored me, spoke over me, and even walked away in the middle of a sentence. It was like I was invisible, and he wasn't even aware that I was in the room. I was furious at him in the dream! When I woke up, I was still fuming at him.

I could have nursed that anger along and stayed irritated, but I took a step back and analyzed the dream for a few minutes. When I thought about what was going on in my life, I realized that there was a situation at work that I hadn't spoken up about—and I should have. It was always on my mind, and I realized the dream was about me, not my husband. I was the one who needed to speak up. I was invisible and ignored in my dream because I was holding my thoughts and opinions inside.

Don't Brag

I have a friend who has been changing dreams for over ten years. This person has seen remarkable results in many areas of life, ranging from family matters to government and political issues to business prospects. I am not allowed to share any of these dreams because they are extremely personal to this person, and they have only shared a small percentage of the dreams they have changed with me.

There are a few reasons not to share everything that God shows us (though I'm sure there are many more).

First, your dreams can develop into a personal love language with God. Use your dreams to build an intimate relationship with the Lord. Talk to Him about them, ask Him questions, study the Word, and listen to what He is saying to you.

Second, if you dream about well-known people, their privacy is vital. It only takes one slip of the tongue to lose trust. Be cautious about who you tell your dreams to and how you talk about them. Ask the Lord for wisdom, and He will direct you. When in doubt, err on the side of silence.

Third, sharing dreams could sound like bragging. Consider Joseph who shared his dreams with his brothers—and landed himself in a heap of trouble. His brothers hated him because of it! Who wouldn't be mad if their kid brother told them they would bow down to him one day? Be discerning and wise about which dreams to talk about—because sharing *all* dreams could come across as gloating. Fortunately, God used Joseph's situation for good, even though his brothers meant it for evil (Genesis 50:20).

Proverbs 17:27–28 tells us, "The one who has knowledge uses words with restraint, and whoever has understanding is even-tempered. Even fools are thought wise if they keep silent, and discerning if they hold their tongues". There is definitely a time to share dreams with others, but it's better to err on the side of sharing less than to blurt everything out.

These are just a few tips on what *not* to do when you change your dreams. Let the Lord guide you as you grow in your authority and wisdom in changing dreams, and you will avoid unnecessary trouble. The good news is that God is merciful, and He will give plenty of opportunities to try again.

10

FINAL THOUGHTS

As you start this journey of discovering the power of changing dreams, I pray that you will find your relationship with the Lord closer than ever before. I hope you discover the excitement that I have found in walking alongside Him on this incredible journey.

The next time you encounter a bad dream or one that you don't understand, don't be discouraged. Always remember this simple truth: if you ask, God will help you with the strategy you need to change these dreams. Once you realize the authority you have in the Lord, you no longer have to be a powerless victim and passive slave to the enemy's harassment.

My prayer for you is that when you have a bad or confusing dream, you will wake up expectant because now you are on the offense, fighting against the plans of the enemy, instead of the defense. May you be confident knowing that though the enemy has tipped his hand, you can join with the Lord to counteract these attacks. And may your dream life be exciting and purposeful as you learn how to transform your nightmares into victories and win spiritual battles in your sleep.

In a dream, a vision of the night, when sound sleep falls on men, while they slumber in their beds, then He opens the ears of men, and seals their instruction.
(Job 33:15–16 NASB)

ENDNOTES

3. Changing Dreams: What Is This?

1. McGill, Cindy, and David Sluka. *What Your Dreams are Telling You; Unlocking Solutions While You Sleep.* Chosen Books, 2013.
2. Price, Paula A. *The Prophet's Dictionary; The Ultimate Guide to Supernatural Wisdom.* Whitaker House, 1999–2006.
3. https://streamsministries.com/shop/understanding-dreams-and-visions/
4. https://www.streamsministries.com/
5. (https://dare2believe.info/)
6. Saunders, Recie. *A Parent's Guide to Understanding Children's Dreams and Nightmares.* Whitaker House, 2017

RECOMMENDED RESOURCES

If you need help changing a dream, we can help! Go to www.bethchiles.net and submit your dream.

John Paul Jackson, *Streams Ministries International* at https://www.streamsministries.com/

Kristi Graner's online class, "Understanding Your Dreams." https://www.understandingyourdreams.org/

Blouin, Annie. *Everlasting Prophetic; Bridging Heaven to Earth.* Life Press, 2016.

Goll, James W., and Michal Ann Goll. *Dream Language; The Prophetic Power of Dreams, Revelations, and the Spirit of Wisdom.* Destiny Image, 2006.

Hamon, Jane. *Dreams & Visions; Understanding and Interpreting God's Messages to You.* Dream Themes Collection. Chosen Books, 2000–2016.

Jackson, John Paul. *Top 20 Dreams; What the Most Common Dreams are Telling You.* Streams Ministries International, 2015.

McGill, Cindy, and David Sluka. *What Your Dreams are Telling You; Unlocking Solutions While You Sleep.* Chosen Books, 2013.

Meyer, Julie. *Dreams & Supernatural Encounters; An Invitation for Everyone to Experience God.* Destiny Image, 2011.

Milligan, Ira. *Understanding the Dreams You Dream; Biblical Keys for Hearing God's Voice in the Night.* Treasure House, 1993–1997.

Price, Paula A. *The Prophet's Dictionary; The Ultimate Guide to Supernatural Wisdom.* Whitaker House, 1999–2006.

Saunders, Recie. *A Parent's Guide to Understanding Children's Dreams and Nightmares.* Whitaker House, 2017.

DREAM CHANGER JOURNAL

The next pages contain a sample of the Dream Changer Journal. Recording your dreams is the first and most essential step in your dream life. Your dream journal will become a treasure trove of memories that grow in depth over time as you record them. It is a powerful way to explore the seasons of your life, gain insight into your destiny, or make corrections in areas you may be struggling in.

The primary difference in this dream journal is the section on changing dreams. If you would like help changing a dream, go to www.bethchiles.net and submit your dream there.

The *Dream Changer Journal* describes each section of the journal in detail, and gives examples of the different kinds of dreams. You can purchase it at my website: www.bethchiles.net.

Dream Changer Journal

DREAM TITLE: DATE & TIME:

Description (location, colors, sounds, objects, characters, emotions) :

Type of Dream:

DIRECTIONAL

WARNING

SPIRITUAL WARFARE

HEALING

NATURAL

Does this dream relate to any past or present situations in your life?

Have you had a similar dream in the past? Compare and contrast.

Does this dream need to be changed?   YES   NO

If yes, how should it be changed?

Prayer points:

Sketch:

Dream Changer Journal

DREAM TITLE: DATE & TIME:

Description (location, colors, sounds, objects, characters, emotions) :

Type of Dream:

DIRECTIONAL

WARNING

SPIRITUAL WARFARE

HEALING

NATURAL

Does this dream relate to any past or present situations in your life?

Have you had a similar dream in the past? Compare and contrast.

Does this dream need to be changed?   YES   NO

If yes, how should it be changed?

Prayer points:

Sketch:

ABOUT THE AUTHOR

Beth Chiles has been studying dreams for over 30 years. She is passionate about helping people overcome their bad dreams and discover their authority in the Lord. Beth lives in Waco, Texas with her husband and two children, who are her greatest joy.

If you need help changing a dream, we can help! Go to www.bethchiles.net and submit your dream.

www.bethchiles.net

Dream Changer Journal

Dream Changer, Large Print

Made in the USA
Middletown, DE
27 January 2021

32506461R00056